IT'S TIME TO EAT ARUGULA

It's Time to Eat ARUGULA

Walter the Educator

Silent King Books
A WhichHead Entertainment Imprint

Copyright © 2025 by Walter the Educator

All rights reserved. No part of this book may be reproduced in any manner whatsoever without written per- mission except in the case of brief quotations embodied in critical articles and reviews.

First Printing, 2024

Disclaimer

This book is a literary work; the story is not about specific persons, locations, situations, and/or circumstances unless mentioned in a historical context. Any resemblance to real persons, locations, situations, and/or circumstances is coincidental. This book is for entertainment and informational purposes only. The author and publisher offer this information without warranties expressed or implied. No matter the grounds, neither the author nor the publisher will be accountable for any losses, injuries, or other damages caused by the reader's use of this book. The use of this book acknowledges an understanding and acceptance of this disclaimer.

It's Time to Eat ARUGULA is a collectible early learning book by Walter the Educator suitable for all ages belonging to Walter the Educator's Time to Eat Book Series. Collect more books at WaltertheEducator.com

USE THE EXTRA SPACE TO TAKE NOTES AND DOCUMENT YOUR MEMORIES

ARUGULA

It's time to eat, hooray, hooray!

It's Time to Eat
Arugula

A tasty green is on the way.

With leaves so crisp and full of might,

Arugula makes each bite just right!

It's leafy, fresh, and full of spice,

A little peppery, a little nice.

It loves to sit upon your plate,

So grab your fork, don't make it wait!

In salads, sandwiches, or more,

It brings a taste we all adore.

So take a bite, and you will see,

How yummy greens can truly be!

It grows outside beneath the sun,

And picking it is so much fun!

The farmers wash it clean and bright,

Then send it off, a tasty sight!

It's Time to Eat
Arugula

Arugula is good for you,

It helps you grow up strong and true.

It gives you energy to play,

To run, to jump, and laugh all day!

Some people like it with a crunch,

Or mixed inside a cheesy lunch.

A drizzle of dressing, maybe some cheese,

Eat it how you like, it's sure to please!

Tiny leaves so dark and green,

Make your plate look fresh and clean.

A rainbow meal is fun to eat,

With colors bright and flavors sweet!

Try one bite, just give it a go,

You might just love it, who will know?

Crunch and munch, enjoy the taste,

It's Time to Eat
Arugula

No arugula should go to waste!

So when it's time to eat today,

Let arugula lead the way.

Healthy, yummy, crisp, and bright,

A tasty green that feels just right!

So grab your fork and take a seat,

Arugula's here, it's time to eat!

A little leaf, so full of cheer,

It's Time to Eat
Arugula

Let's eat and smile from ear to ear!

ABOUT THE CREATOR

Walter the Educator is one of the pseudonyms for Walter Anderson. Formally educated in Chemistry, Business, and Education, he is an educator, an author, a diverse entrepreneur, and he is the son of a disabled war veteran. "Walter the Educator" shares his time between educating and creating. He holds interests and owns several creative projects that entertain, enlighten, enhance, and educate, hoping to inspire and motivate you. Follow, find new works, and stay up to date with Walter the Educator™ at WaltertheEducator.com

www.ingramcontent.com/pod-product-compliance
Lightning Source LLC
LaVergne TN
LVHW052010060526
838201LV00059B/3954